D0754953

KINGFISHER

Kingfisher Publication Plc
New Penderel House
283–288 High Holborn
London WC1V 7HZ
www.kingfisherpub.com

First published by Kingfisher Publications Plc in 2005
4 6 8 10 9 7 5 3
3TR/0106/TIMS/PICA/128MA/F

Managing editor: Russell Mclean
Designer and picture researcher: Dominic Zwemmer
Illustrators: Mike Buckley, Malcolm Parchment
Picture research manager: Cee Weston-Baker
DTP coordinator: Susanne Olbrich
Production controller: Jessamy Oldfield
Indexer: Jennie Morris

Note to readers: The website addresses listed in this book are correct at the time
of publishing. However, due to the ever-changing nature of the internet, website
addresses and content can change. Websites can contain links that are unsuitable
for children. The publisher cannot be held responsible for changes in website
addresses or content, or for information obtained through third-party websites.
We strongly advise that internet searches should be supervised by an adult.

The publisher would like to thank the following for permission to reproduce their
material. Every care has been taken to trace copyright holders. However, if there
have been unintentional omissions or failure to trace copyright holders, we apologize
and will, if informed, endeavour to make corrections in any future edition.

Cover: Corbis/Dusko Despotovic; pages 3, 7, 13, 17, 21, 25, 27, 29, 30, 33, 35,
39 and 45 Empics/PA; pages 6 and 23 Corbis/Reuters; page 31 Getty Images Sport

Cover image: this image in no way indicates any endorsement or affiliation by David
Beckham, his representatives, any individuals or organizations connected to him.

A CIP catalogue record is available from the British Library.

ISBN-13: 978 0 7534 1244 2
ISBN-10: 0 7534 1244 6

Printed in China

Football Skills

Football **Skills**

Clive Gifford

KINGFISHER

Contents

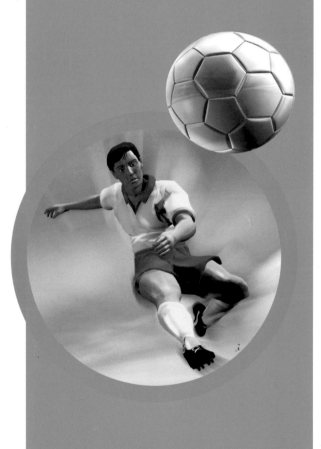

Kick-off

Football is the world's number one team sport, and with good reason. It is a thrilling, all-action game, played and watched by millions of people. The top players are worldwide superstars. But everyone can enjoy improving their skills – and helping their side to win matches.

Ready to play

Always warm up before a game by running, skipping, doing star jumps and jogging with your heels almost touching your bottom. This gets your blood moving round your body. After a warm-up, stretch your muscles to help stop injuries. Always hold a stretch for a few seconds, and repeat it several times.

▲ Side stretch

This is a side stretch. Stand with your feet apart and reach smoothly down one side as far as you can. Hold the stretch, then repeat it, stretching your other side.

▲ Thigh stretch

This move stretches your thigh muscles. Pull back your leg smoothly and hold the position as you count to ten.

Kitted up

For a proper game, wear a sports shirt, shorts and long football socks. Strap shinpads round your lower legs to protect them from kicks. Wear a football boot made of soft leather. It must fit comfortably and support your ankle. You will also need a water bottle and a tracksuit to stay warm when you are not playing.

◄ Superstar striker
Ukrainian striker Andriy
Shevchenko plays in Italy for
AC Milan. Here, he jumps to
bring the ball under control.
You can read more about
ball control on pages 12–13.

Top tips

- Always keep your
  kit and boots in
  top condition.
- If your boots have
  screw-in studs, check
  that each stud is
  tight before a game.
- When you are
  training or playing,
  take small drinks
  of water often.

Pitch and players

The pitch is where it all happens. For a full game, it measures around 100m long and 65–70m wide. Each side has 11 players, who usually line up in banks of defenders, midfielders and attackers (see page 38). They play two halves of 45 minutes, plus any time for injury or other stoppages. During the game, the coach or manager of a team can replace one or more players with substitutes.

▲ Corner
A goal kick or a corner is given when the ball goes over the goal line. Here, the referee's assistant signals for a corner.

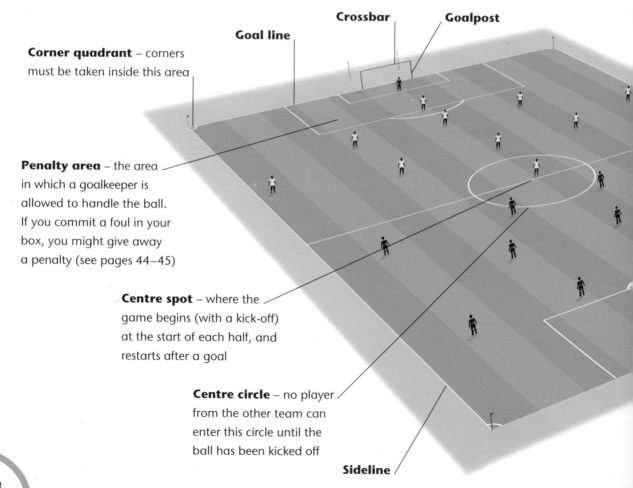

Corner quadrant – corners must be taken inside this area

Goal line

Crossbar

Goalpost

Penalty area – the area in which a goalkeeper is allowed to handle the ball. If you commit a foul in your box, you might give away a penalty (see pages 44–45)

Centre spot – where the game begins (with a kick-off) at the start of each half, and restarts after a goal

Centre circle – no player from the other team can enter this circle until the ball has been kicked off

Sideline

Ball in play

Ball out of play

Goal

No goal

No goal

No goal

Goal or no goal?
For a goal to be allowed by the referee, the whole of the ball must cross the line between the goalposts. Here, only the ball at the very top is a goal.

In or out of play?
When the ball is on the pitch, it is said to be in play. When it leaves the pitch, it is out of play. For a ball to be out of play, the whole of the ball has to cross the line.

Halfway line – divides the pitch into two equal-sized areas of play. Players have to stay in their own half before a kick-off

Penalty spot – from where penalties are taken

Goal area – the area in which goal kicks must be taken

▶ Throw-in
When the ball goes out of play on the sidelines, the referee's assistant signals for a throw-in. He points his flag towards the goal that the throwing-in team is attacking.

Referees and rules

The referee and the assistants run the game. They judge whether the ball has gone out of play and which team touched it last. The referee blows a whistle to stop the game if a player is caught offside or commits a foul. Fouls include handball, pushing, tripping or kicking an opponent, shirt-pulling and bad language. Referees award free kicks or a penalty if a serious foul happens inside the penalty area.

Advantage

If you are fouled in a good position, the referee can choose to let the game run instead of giving a free kick. It is called playing advantage. This is the referee's signal for it.

Yellow and red

A yellow card is a warning. If you get two yellow cards in one game or commit a very serious offence, such as a dangerous foul, you are shown a red card. You have to leave the pitch and are out of the game. Your team must carry on with one less player.

▲ Foul
This player has committed a deliberate and dangerous foul to stop a striker who has a clear chance of scoring. The referee often shows a red card for this type of foul.

Offside

When a team-mate passes the ball forwards, two opposition players must be either level with you or between you and the opponent's goal. If not, the referee may blow for offside and give the other team a free kick. The offside rule does not count if:

- you are behind the ball when it is kicked;

- you receive the ball directly from a throw-in, a corner or a goal kick;

- you are in your own half of the pitch;

- in the referee's opinion, you are not involved in play or gaining an advantage.

Signal for offside

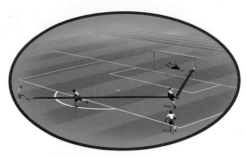

▲ Offside

The goal scorer is offside when the ball is played to him. The goal is not given and the other team gets a free kick.

▲ Not offside

The scorer is in front of the goalkeeper, but there are two defenders between him and the goal. He is not offside.

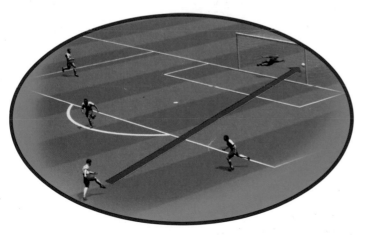

▲ Not involved

The player in yellow and red (just inside the penalty area) is not involved in play when his team-mate shoots. The referee awards the goal.

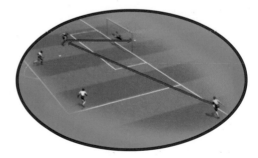

▲ Not offside

You are not offside if you are behind the ball when it is played. Here, the scorer is not offside and the goal is allowed by the referee.

Ball control

A football can zip around the pitch at great speed. Cushioning helps you get the ball under control. Keep your body relaxed and balanced. As the ball arrives, move the part of your body that will make contact back or down in the direction in which the ball is moving. This slows the ball and stops it bouncing away.

Ball trapping

Trapping is a way to control a rolling ball. Use the sole of your boot to hold the ball firmly. Do not stamp on the ball, or it might pop out from under your foot.

Sidefoot cushion

1 A sidefoot cushion is a good way to control a ball that is skidding across the pitch. Move your weight onto your standing foot, using your arms for balance.

2 As the ball arrives, lift your leg and try to bring the ball down with the side of your foot.

Thigh cushion

You can cushion a high, falling ball with your thigh. Raise your upper leg so that it is almost parallel to the ground. As the ball arrives, pull your leg down to cushion it. Try to drop the ball in front of your feet.

3 The ball should drop to the ground, ready for you to make a pass to another player. You could also run with the ball or take a shot.

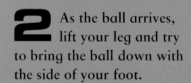
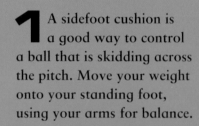

Chest cushion

Here, Germany's Michael Ballack controls a high ball with his chest. First, move your feet wide apart for balance. As the ball arrives, lean back to cushion it. When it drops in front of you, put your foot on the ball to get it under control.

Top tips

- As the ball arrives, get into position as soon as you can. Keep your eye on the ball.
- Start moving the part of your body that will cushion the ball just before the ball makes contact.
- When the ball drops, get it under control with your feet as quickly as you can.

Instep cushion

You can also cushion a falling ball with the top part of your boot, where the laces are. This is called the instep. Lift your foot, with your toes pointing slightly down. As the ball arrives, move your foot down towards the ground.

1 The inside of your foot makes sidefoot passes.

2 Make short flicks and hit long crosses and shots with the outside of your foot.

3 Hit instep passes and shots with the top of your boot, where the laces are.

Passing

Passing is the most important skill to master. It links players all over the pitch and allows a team to build attacks. Practise your passing as often as you can by copying the top players. Work especially hard with your weaker foot. A player who can pass well with both feet is often a match winner.

Sidefoot pass

You can use the inside of the foot to make a sidefoot or push pass. This is the simplest pass, and it is the easiest to control because more of your boot touches the ball than with any other pass. It is used to hit the ball over short or medium distances and for close shots on goal.

1 Position your body over the ball, with your standing foot beside it.

2 Swing your leg and push through the middle of the ball with the inside of your foot.

3 Follow through smoothly, keeping your eye on the ball as you pass.

Circle passing

Getting your passes on target is crucial. Try this fun passing drill, with four players standing round the edge of the centre circle and another player in the middle. The middle player receives a pass. Then he turns and hits an accurate sidefoot pass so that the person who gets the ball does not have to move to control it.

◀ Pressure pass
Under pressure from an opponent, this player has made a good sidefoot pass. His foot has followed through and is pointing in the direction in which the ball is travelling.

Longer passing

The instep pass is the most common pass for hitting the ball over longer distances. You can use it for shots, too. Position your body over the ball, with your non-kicking foot beside it. Point your toes down and aim to hit the middle of the ball with your boot laces. Keep your foot stretched and your toes pointing down as you swing your leg smoothly through the ball. Your foot should end up pointing in the direction of the pass.

Lofted instep drive

This is similar to an instep pass, but it sends the ball higher and longer. Use it for crosses and to make clearances out of defence.

▶ Pass star

The USA's Brandi Chastain hits a long instep pass on the move. Vary how far a pass travels by taking a longer or shorter swing of your leg and by moving your kicking leg faster or slower.

1 Your standing foot should be placed to the side and slightly behind the ball. Swing your kicking leg smoothly, with your toes pointing down.

2 Aim to hit the bottom half of the ball. Lean back slightly, as this helps to send the ball higher. Keep your eye on the ball.

3 After hitting the ball, your foot should follow through and move slightly across your body. Practise hitting this pass with different amounts of force.

Three against one

To practise instep and sidefoot passing under pressure, mark out a small area with four cones. A team of three players has to pass the ball without a fourth player getting it. When the ball leaves the area or the fourth player gets the ball, he switches with one of the team of three.

Top tips
- Check your target just before you make a pass.
- Try to hit the ball smoothly, with the right amount of force.
- Use the sidefoot pass for shorter passing. Use the instep drive for longer passing.
- Work on all types of pass with both feet. Practise passing and receiving the ball with your friends.

Movement and space

Once you have made a pass, don't stand there and admire it – get moving. You should be looking for space on the pitch in which you can receive a pass from a team-mate. Quick, accurate passing and moving between two or more players can open up a game and move the ball down the pitch very quickly.

Player 1

▶ One-two pass

A simple but very useful passing move is the one-two pass, or wall pass. Here, player 1 passes to a team-mate. He then sprints past the opponent in red and receives a quick return pass ahead of him. The pass cuts out the defender.

Triangle passing

Practise your passing and moving using the game on page 17 and also with this triangles drill. With two team-mates, pass and move your way up and down a pitch. When you get the ball, make a short, accurate pass. Then sprint into space to receive the ball again.

Passing and moving

Football is a fast-changing game. A brilliant position to receive a pass may be blocked in an instant. So, when you are looking to receive a pass, be alert and ready to move. Making quick passes on the move is a tricky skill. Usually, you cannot aim at where the player is, but at where you think he will be when the ball arrives. You need to judge how fast your team-mate is moving and how far away he is.

Player 1

Decoy run

A decoy is when a player moves as if he wants to receive the ball but is, in fact, trying to make space for a team-mate. At this throw-in, player 1 has moved towards the thrower and a defender has followed him. This has created space further up the pitch for a team-mate to run into and receive the throw.

Five-a-side

Play a five-a-side game to practise your passing and moving skills. Here, a player beats an opponent by using the wall of the pitch to make a one-two pass to himself.

1 The attacker is blocked in by two defenders.

2 He plays the ball against the wall...

3 ... and collects the rebound.

Dribbling, shielding and turning

When you run with the ball and try to beat defenders, it is called dribbling. Keep the ball close to you and under control at all times. As you move, tap the ball forwards with the inside and outside of your feet. To beat opponents you will also need to be able to shield the ball, turn and feint.

Feinting

Feinting is pretending to turn one way to fool an opponent, before turning another way.

1 The dribbling player (in red) feints to turn right. He leans to the right and drops his right shoulder.

2 The defender lunges to the attacker's right.

3 The dribbler fools the defender by turning to the left and dribbling past.

Shielding

1 Shielding is a way to keep the ball when you are under pressure. This player has received a pass just as an opponent closes in quickly.

2 He shields the ball by putting his body between it and the opponent. He must keep the ball under close control and stay on the move.

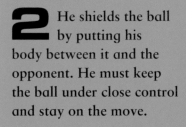

3 While shielding the ball, he must not push or foul his opponent. He looks for his next move and makes a sidefoot pass to a team-mate.

◀ Star dribbler
Manchester United's Wayne Rooney dribbles through a packed defence. He is nicely balanced and has his eye on the ball as he makes a sharp turn.

Outside hook

One way to turn with the ball is to use an outside hook. Lean in the direction you want to turn and hook the outside of your foot around the ball. Swivel on your standing foot and drag the ball with you as you turn.

Volleying and shooting

When you shoot, there is no point in kicking the ball really hard if your shot is not on target. Near the goal, you can shoot with a strong sidefoot pass (see page 15). From further away, try an instep pass (see page 16).

Volley

Kicking the ball when it is in the air is called a volley. Use it to clear the ball a long distance or to hit a powerful shot.

1 To hit a front-on volley, lift your knee as the ball comes near. Then swing your leg with your toes pointing down.

2 Make contact with the ball on your boot laces. Remember to keep your head over the ball.

Half volley

A half volley is when the ball is struck just after it has hit the ground. Stretch your ankle so that your toes point at the ground. Keep your body over the ball so that it stays down after you kick it.

▶ **Side volley**
Michael Owen hits a powerful sidefoot volley for his club, Real Madrid. His leg is parallel to the ground and he is watching the ball closely.

Shoot

Practise your shooting by marking out four squares on a wall with chalk. Ask a friend to pass the ball to you, then aim for each of the squares in turn.

Heading

Heading does not hurt when you use the right technique. If you are nervous of heading, practise with a soft ball to build up your skills. Start with headers from a standing position, with one foot behind the other and your knees bent. This gives you a stable base.

1 As the ball travels through the air, pull your upper body and head back a little. Remember to keep your eyes open.

2 Push your head forwards to meet the ball with the middle of your forehead. Keep your neck muscles firm to help direct the ball away.

Heading down

For most headers, you will be trying to get slightly over the ball in order to direct it downwards to a team-mate's feet or towards the goal. Practise downward headers with this heading drill. After five headers in a row, swap positions with your partner.

1 One player gently lobs the ball up to his partner with an underarm throw.

2 The other player heads the ball down to the feet of the thrower.

Defensive header

Defenders often have to direct powerful headers up and away from their penalty area. When you are clearing the ball away from danger, head the ball at the top of your jump. Try to get plenty of distance and height on your header.

Heading goals

Many goals are scored by headers, especially from corners or crosses into the goal area. This attacker has jumped high to get his head above the ball. He guides it down into the corner of the goal, giving the goalkeeper no chance.

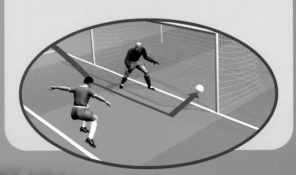

▶ Power header

For maximum distance and force, you need to make a power header. Here, the Republic of Ireland's Robbie Keane springs forwards to meet the ball in mid-air. He thrusts his arms back to help drive his neck and head forwards to meet the ball.

Tackling

All players have to tackle, not just defenders. Tackles are best made when you have team-mates nearby as cover, but sometimes you have no choice but to make a tackle to stop a goal chance. Tackling requires perfect timing. Once you decide to make a tackle, go for it firmly and keep your eye on the ball. Try to stay on your feet. This allows you to pass the ball if you get it or chase back if your tackle is unsuccessful.

Front block tackle

The most common tackles are called block tackles because you use your foot to block the path of the ball and force it away from your opponent.

1 The player in white bends his knees, ready to make the tackle.

2 He uses the inside of his boot to make firm contact with the middle of the ball.

3 If the ball gets stuck, he tries to roll the ball over or flick it away from the opponent's foot.

4 When the ball is free, he moves away to get the ball under control.

Clearing the ball

Sometimes, winning a tackle in your penalty area gives you time to choose who to pass to. At other times, you may be under pressure at once. This is when you should hit a long, quick clearance.

◀ Perfect timing

Brazilian defender Cafu (in white) moves in to kick the ball away from winger Cristiano Ronaldo during a Champions League game. To make tackles and interceptions, you have to time your challenge well.

Playing in goal

Goalkeepers are the only players on the pitch who are allowed to handle the ball – but only inside their own penalty area. Much of the time, a keeper can keep his goal safe by staying alert and giving intructions to his defenders. When the other team attacks, he should stand on the balls of his feet with his legs apart and his knees bent. This allows the keeper to move quickly – to run out to meet the ball with a kick or a catch, or to dive to one side to make a save.

Narrowing the angle

1 An attacker has the ball and is running towards the goal. The keeper reacts by coming off the goal line and moving towards the attacker. He is narrowing the angle.

2 The keeper stays upright as he closes in on the attacker. He tries to block as much of the goal as possible to the attacker's view. This makes it harder to score.

- Get your body behind a ball that you are trying to stop or catch.
- Watch the ball all the way into your hands.
- Pay attention to the game and talk to your team-mates.
- If you decide to go for a ball in a crowded penalty area, call loudly and go for it.

Gathering the ball

To collect a low ball, drop down onto one knee and lean forwards with your body in line with the ball's direction. Gather the ball and scoop it up into your body to keep it safe.

3 The keeper dives for the ball at the feet of the attacker. He spreads himself, gets his hands on the ball and gathers it in quickly to his body.

▶ Safe catch

German goalkeeper Oliver Kahn takes a catch above his head. To hold the ball safely, his hands are behind the ball to either side.

29

Stunning saves

Sometimes, a goalkeeper has to leap across the goal to make a spectacular save. Keepers catch the ball whenever they can, but if that is not possible they try to tip the ball over the crossbar or push it round the post. In a crowded penalty area, a keeper may choose to punch the ball away firmly to clear it from danger.

▲ Brave save

Keepers must be ready at all times to come off their line to stop an attack. They have to be brave, too. Here, Petr Cech dives at the feet of an attacker to get the ball.

Making a diving save

1 Standing on the balls of his feet, the keeper starts to move across the goal.

2 He pushes off from one foot to start diving to his left. He tries to keep his eyes on the ball.

3 He stretches out his arms and gets his hands behind the ball with his fingers spread.

4 He gathers the ball into his chest and protects it from spilling out as he lands.

Releasing the ball

After making a save, a keeper has six seconds to release the ball. A long kick up the pitch or a quick throw to a team-mate in lots of space can help to start an attack. Goalkeepers have to be able to kick a rolling ball well because of the backpass rule. When a team-mate uses his feet to pass the ball back to the keeper, he cannot pick it up. Instead, the keeper must head the ball or kick it clear.

◄ Underarm throw
Norway's Bente Nordby has spotted a team-mate in lots of space and is rolling the ball out underarm. After releasing the ball, her arm will follow through to point at her target.

Attacking skills

Teams attack in many different ways. They can quickly turn defence into attack by winning the ball and hitting a long pass to a striker who has stayed up the pitch. They can cross the ball into the penalty area or chip the ball over opponents into space. They can also build an attack patiently by using lots of short passes.

Crosses

A cross is a pass from out wide into the penalty area. Look up to see where your team-mates are, then hit the ball with plenty of pace. This attacker has used a lofted instep drive (see page 16) to hit a high cross, aiming for the head of a team-mate near the goal.

Chipping

A chip is a pass or shot that rises steeply into the air. You can use it to carry the ball over the head of a defender to a team-mate who is in lots of space. A chip can also beat a keeper who is a long way off the goal line.

1 To hit a chip, you need to strike the bottom of the ball.

2 Use a strong downwards stab of your foot to make contact.

3 Keep your follow-through short. The ball should rise steeply into the air.

Push and go

In some attacking situations, you can beat a defender not by dribbling but by making a pass to yourself. This is called a push and go. Carefully push a pass beyond the defender. As soon as the ball leaves your foot, sprint hard to collect the ball.

▼ Quick control

Arsenal's Thierry Henry uses his great pace to push the ball ahead and sprint past a defender. He has moved the ball ahead of him a little way, but not so far that he cannot regain control of it quickly.

Opening up defences

It often gets crowded in and around the penalty area you are attacking. Space can be hard to find and you may be marked closely by an opposition player. When you are running towards goal, make a sudden change of direction and pace to get away from your marker and into space for a pass. One top tip is to lean and take a step in one direction. Then swivel on one foot and sprint away in another direction.

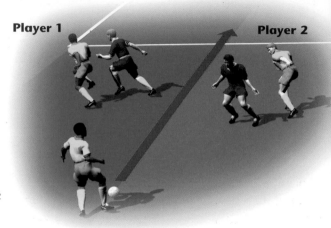

Player 1   Player 2

Making space

You can create space for a team-mate to attack by running in one direction and taking your marker with you. Here, player 1 has sprinted to the left. This has left a gap, which player 2 will run into to receive a pass.

Overlap

You can use the full width of the pitch to create extra space for an attack. An attacker who runs down the sideline ahead of the ball creates an overlap.

1 The attacker is near the edge of the pitch. As he gets near to the defender in red, he passes to a team-mate.

2 The defender is caught in two minds. This allows the attacker to run down the line.

3 The attacker receives a return pass. He may be able to hit a cross or run with the ball towards goal.

Backheel

Sometimes, a backheel in a crowded penalty area can fool opponents and give a team-mate a chance to have a shot. Strike through the middle of the ball with your heel or the sole of your boot.

Through balls

Through balls are attacking passes that travel behind opposition defenders. Here, player 1 has played the ball ahead of player 2 (the receiver) so that he can run onto the ball. A through pass has to be hit with the right amount of weight for the receiver to be able to reach it.

Top tips

- A good way to create attacking openings is to pass the ball quickly between players with as few touches as possible. Practise one- and two-touch passing moves with your friends.
- If your team has a shot on goal, follow the ball in. Be alert in case it rebounds towards you.
- Do not be afraid to have a shot if you are in the penalty area and you cannot see a better option.

Player 2

Player 1

Defending

Defending may not be as exciting as attacking and scoring goals, but it is just as important. When your team loses the ball, the whole side must defend to stop the opposition scoring and to win the ball back. Try to get between the ball and your goal, filling up space that the other side may want to attack in. You should mark and cover opponents as they make attacking runs.

Interception

All players must work hard to win back the ball for their side. This alert striker (in blue) has spotted a weak pass and has intercepted the ball.

◀ Two against one

Two Sparta Prague defenders work together to challenge Lyon's Sydney Govou. One defender stays in support as his team-mate (on the right) prepares to make a tackle.

▲ Slowing down

A defender (in blue shorts) is jockeying an attacker who has his back towards goal. This gives his side time to get into a good defensive position.

Jockeying

Delaying a player who has the ball is called jockeying. Close in on the opponent until you are 1–2m away. Stand on the balls of your feet, with knees bent and arms out for balance. Try to stay between your goal and the other player, slowing him down. If a team-mate arrives to cover you, try to make a tackle to win the ball.

Top tips

- Talk to your team-mates and defend together.
- Do not dive into a tackle unless team-mates are behind you as cover.
- Jockey an opponent who has the ball to slow him down as much as possible.
- If you are man-to-man marking a player, stay with him at all times. Do not get distracted.
- When you clear the ball out of defence, do it quickly and safely.

Marking

The defender in blue is man-to-man marking an attacker. He stays close to the attacker, giving him less time and space to get the ball. Man-to-man markers try to stay between the player they are marking and their own goal.

Tactics

Tactics are the way in which a team chooses to play a match, and also its plans for winning it. Tactics can involve using special moves – such as corners and free kicks, which can be practised in training – or marking a particularly dangerous opponent throughout the game. Managers can change tactics during a match, depending on how it is going.

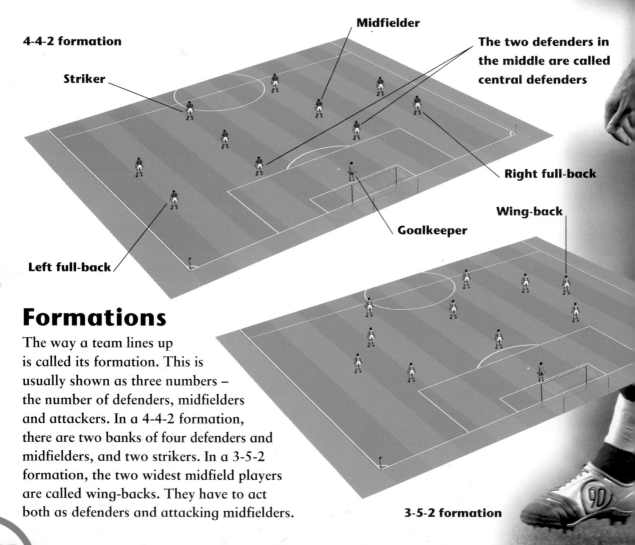

4-4-2 formation

Striker

Midfielder

The two defenders in the middle are called central defenders

Right full-back

Wing-back

Goalkeeper

Left full-back

Formations

The way a team lines up is called its formation. This is usually shown as three numbers – the number of defenders, midfielders and attackers. In a 4-4-2 formation, there are two banks of four defenders and midfielders, and two strikers. In a 3-5-2 formation, the two widest midfield players are called wing-backs. They have to act both as defenders and attacking midfielders.

3-5-2 formation

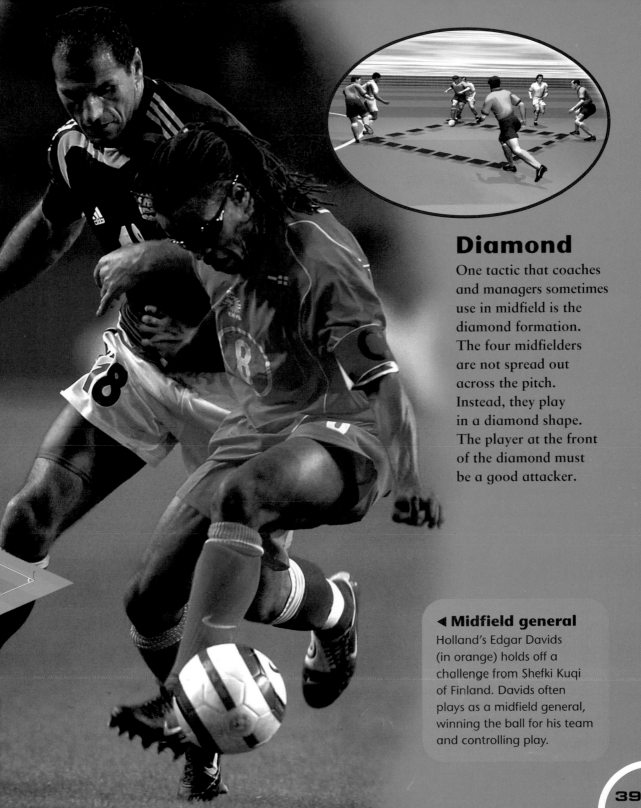

Diamond

One tactic that coaches and managers sometimes use in midfield is the diamond formation. The four midfielders are not spread out across the pitch. Instead, they play in a diamond shape. The player at the front of the diamond must be a good attacker.

◄ Midfield general

Holland's Edgar Davids (in orange) holds off a challenge from Shefki Kuqi of Finland. Davids often plays as a midfield general, winning the ball for his team and controlling play.

Throw-ins and corners

When the ball goes out of play, the referee will signal for a throw-in, a corner or a goal kick. A throw-in is given when the ball runs over the sideline. When you take a throw-in, both feet must be on the ground behind the sideline and both hands must be on the ball. Corners are awarded when the ball crosses the goal line and the defending team touched it last.

◄ Throw-in grip
Spread your hands around the back and sides of the ball so that your thumbs almost touch. This gives you a good grip on the ball.

Throw-in

To take a throw-in, bring the ball back behind your head, then bend your back and bring your hands forwards. Let go of the ball just before your arms come over your head.

► Return pass
Once you have taken a throw-in, step back onto the pitch in case the player who receives the throw passes the ball straight back to you.

Corners

This player is aiming to hit a corner into the goal area. When you strike a corner, make sure you are well balanced on your standing leg and hit through the middle of the ball. Your kicking leg should follow through and across your body.

Top tips

- When you take a corner, aim for a target just above head height.
- Make sure you are completely balanced on your non-kicking foot.
- Strike the ball hard enough to carry it into the penalty area.
- Surprise your opponents by hitting a short corner from time to time.

Corner choices

At a corner, attacking players look for a ball that is crossed high into the goal area. If you aim a corner at the post nearest to you (yellow arrow), an attacker can flick the ball on with his head. If you aim for the middle of the goal area (red arrow), an attacker may hit a volley shot.

Free kicks

When a referee blows the whistle for offside, a bad tackle or another kind of foul, he will usually award a free kick to one team. The ball is placed on the ground and the opposition side must move back 9m. There are two types of free kick.

Signal for an indirect free kick

Signal for a direct free kick

◀ Direct or indirect
You can score straight from a direct free kick. With an indirect free kick, you must play the ball to a team-mate.

Attacking free kicks

Free kicks in front of and quite close to the other team's goal offer your side a chance to score. Defending teams often put up a wall of their players to block a straight shot on goal. You have to find a way round that wall.

Skilful players may try to bend or swerve the ball round or over the wall

Defensive wall

A pass to this player may give him a clear shot on goal

Top tips

- When you take a free kick in the middle of the pitch, a short, quick pass can often release a team-mate.
- Do not try to blast a shot from a free kick when you are a long way from goal. Instead, make a pass or cross the ball into the penalty area.
- Vary your free kicks throughout a game. This keeps the other side guessing.

Bending the ball

To hit an outside swerve, kick through the side of the ball with the outside of your boot. As you follow through, your foot should move across your body. To hit an inside swerve, kick low through the side of the ball with the inside of your foot. Your follow-through should be straight.

Outside swerve

43

Penalties

If there is a deliberate handball or a serious foul in the penalty area, the referee will award a free shot on goal. This is called a penalty. Only the penalty taker and the goalkeeper are allowed in the penalty area during the tense moments leading up to the kick. But team-mates stand round the edge of the area, ready to race in if the shot rebounds off the keeper, the goalposts or the crossbar.

Taking a penalty

1 Think positively before you step up to take a penalty. Decide where you are going to aim the ball. Then begin your run-up, keeping your eye on the ball, not the keeper.

2 Keep your head down and your body balanced as you hit the ball. This player tries to trick the keeper by looking as if he will kick the ball to the right. Instead, he aims left.

3 The penalty taker hits a firm sidefoot pass low into the corner of the goal. He has beaten the keeper, who dived the wrong way. He scores!

Penalty practice

Aim practice penalties between the goalposts and two cones. Hit the ball low if you are not experienced at taking penalties. Different players take penalties in different ways. Some blast the ball as hard as they can. Others use a firm sidefoot pass for more accuracy.

▼ Shootout save
Some drawn matches are settled by a penalty shootout. Here, AC Milan goalkeeper Dida makes a save during a shootout in the 2003 Champions League final.

Top tips
- Before you take a penalty, decide how and where you are going to hit it.
- Relax, and think only about getting your shot on target. Aim for the corners of the goal.
- If you miss a penalty, do not worry. Put it out of your mind and carry on playing. Remember, even the greatest players miss penalties.